Life after Dubai

CARMEN LÓPEZ

The information presented herein represents the view of the author as of the date of publication. This book is a memoir and work of creative non-fiction. It reflects the author's recollections of experiences over time and the author's interpretation of conversations that took place. This book contains the personal opinions, viewpoints and ideas of the author. The author has no intention to hurt anyone's feelings by expressing her views. To protect the privacy of individuals, some names, characters, events and identifiable characteristics have been changed, invented, altered, compressed or recreated for literary effect. The reader should consider this book a work of literature. The opinions expressed within this book are the author's personal opinions and are merely 'freedom of expression'.

DEDICATION

To my husband, who has always been supportive and confident in my
ability to get this done.

To my parents, who have always believed in me and have always
encouraged me to follow my dreams.

And to all adventurers, who have left their homelands at some point of
their lives.

CONTENTS

PRELUDE

Living in Dubai has been the most incredible experience I have ever lived by far in a personal and professional way. I was twenty-six years old when I decided to move there, and my dad having only passed away a few months before that. At that time, I was unemployed, and I didn't have a clear idea of what I wanted to do with my life.

Before Dubai I had a few jobs in Barcelona after moving back from London, but I could barely reach the end of the month and the everyday routine was killing me. I was feeling lost. So, when the opportunity of having a completely brand-new life, far away from home came, I didn't doubt it for a second. I was living the best life in Dubai: I was working as a Flight Attendant for one of the world's best airlines and I was living in the most comfortable city in the world. But as they say, it's not gold everything that shines, so it didn't take me to long to understand what the toll was and the price I had to pay, in exchange for this luxury life-style.

After eight years living in a spiral of non-stop travelling alone, paired with the downsides of living in a Muslim country. I started falling apart. Even though the economic situation in Spain was terrible at that time, I was determined to go back home. My surprise was that when I finally managed to escape from the golden cage, when I got back home, I did not recognize 'home' as such, as I was feeling more like a tourist in my own city. Everything and everyone were different and had changed a lot. But maybe, I was the one that changed.

I invite you to read my story, because in order to understand how my life after Dubai is, you must understand how it was before.

1 LIFE BEFORE DUBAI

I've always been attracted to travelling, discovering new places and meeting new people even from a very young age. I guess you either have it or you don't.

My first experience abroad was at the age of nineteen while I was studying in my second year at university. I was offered an internship with a cruise ship company as Sea Stewardess. That was a very exciting experience for me, as it was the first time that I was living by myself without my parents. The funniest thing about the job was that all the workers were living and working together aboard for three months, it was like living on the Big Brother show. I still remember how once a week, my whole family used to come to the Port of Barcelona with my laundry. Unfortunately, I didn't know how to use a washing machine and I was ashamed of asking my colleagues how to use it.

Apart from struggling with my daily chores, I was also stressed with the fact that there was no contact most of the time, as when cruising there wasn't any signal. And at that time, nobody had a mobile phone and Wi-Fi connections didn't exist yet. That first summer experience lasted for three months as I had to go back to university. However, after this amazing experience aboard, I felt that something in me had changed. I was not the same person afterwards and I was left wanting more. And the funny thing was, that another trainee from the cruise who was also studying at the same university as I was, was feeling the same way as I did. So, we decided that the next summer we would start a new adventure together and move to London in order to improve our English level.

When my friend Violet and I moved to London, for the first couple of days we stayed in a cheap hostel in the *Earl's Court* area until we had found a job and a proper place to live. I have to say that our first days there were tough, but at the same time, it was fun not knowing what path our lives

1

would take. In the mornings we would drop our résumé's to every single pub and restaurant in zone one and during the afternoons, we would be calling to all room rental ads that we would find in the daily free newspaper. We got lucky, as in less than a week we found a job and a house to live in.

Our London adventure lasted for no longer than a year as we hadn't finished university yet and we still had exams to take for a couple subjects, to be able to graduate. It was a wonderful experience overall as it was the first time that we had met people from other countries, and we learned about their culture and way of living. Our boss was from Scotland, our landlord was from India, our housemates were from South Africa and our best friends were from Italy. In the pub where we worked as Bartenders, there were also guys from Australia, Sweden and Finland. I thought the Australians were cool people as the only thing I knew about Australia was a TV show called *Heartbreak High*. So, meeting Australian people was very exotic for me. Same as if I had met an alien in a UFO.

If you've ever lived in a foreign country, even if it was only for a couple of months, you would agree with me that living in a foreign country is not the same as going to a foreign country on vacation. When you find out the magic that you experience when you live with other cultures, it is very difficult to go back to your roots.

After we came back from London, I was living the life that anybody in their twenties would have lived. However, I felt bored and trapped in a routine that was filled with everything but excitement. It felt like I was in the movie *Groundhog Day* as every single day was exactly the same: I would get up at seven in the morning, I would walk the dog, I would go to work, I would get back from work, I would go to buy some groceries, I would cook dinner and I would go to sleep early as I had to get up early the next day. Apparently, everyone had the same routine, but no one would complaint about it. Everyone except my friend Mary.

Mary was working as a Flight Attendant and she was flying for a major Spanish airline. Her job was basically to travel to beach destinations in South America, drink mojitos and sleep in beautiful hotels. Plus, her salary was higher than anyone doing an office job! Her life seemed to be just perfect to me. So, suddenly I saw it clear…

I wanted to become a Flight Attendant too!

2 "ARM DOORS AND CROSS CHECK"

"How come someone from sunny Barcelona would want to live and work in England, where we always have this horrendous weather?"

This was one of the questions that the airline recruiter asked me during my interview, when he realized I was from Spain. He couldn't understand why someone from a sunny country would want to leave their family and friends, and move to England, where the weather is depressive and the main sport that you can do is lifting pints in a pub. The recruiter also couldn't understand why someone from a country where you can go to the beach, eat paella and party until six in the morning, would want to live in the depressive town of Crawley.

But what the recruiter didn't know was, how good it feels when you live abroad, as every single day of your life is a new challenge where you can live amazing experiences. And to be honest, Barcelona and my family would always be there waiting for me. And to top it off there, was the fantastic opportunity to start a professional career as Cabin Crew flying to new places for free, what else could I ask for?

I don't remember exactly what where my exact words to his question, but after I answered, he smiled to me and in that precise moment, I knew I had gotten the job. And this is how I started my very first job as Cabin Crew member.

Flying for a commercial airline was cool. But despite a four-day trip to Dublin and a week in the Maldives, I was mostly doing short haul flights to Spain and I was only seeing the sun from the back stairs of the aircraft. As the recruiter kind of advised me. The Maldives trip had been the best layover I have ever done in my cabin crew career, as it was a nine-day charter flight were we basically were staying at the same hotel resort as our passengers. With the difference that we were getting paid just for being there, and the passengers would have to pay lots of money for just a week. I didn't really learn what the meaning of a Flight Attendant was until I did that trip. Most of the people would think that being a trolley dolly is all about offering chicken or beef, pointing the emergency exits, closing and opening doors, or wearing a sexy pair of heels when you are walking through the airport. But being Cabin Crew also means, getting paid for sunbathing in a five star's resort in the Maldives for eight nights in a row. Or at least, this was what I aimed for.

I remember when I saw the Maldives trip in my flight roster. I could not believe it! My flat mate John had had the flight a few weeks before me and he had told me all the cool things you could do on the layover like scuba diving in the mornings and singing at the karaoke bar in the evenings. It was my first time operating a long-haul flight and it was also my first-time experiencing jet lag!

For the lucky ones that don't know what jet lag is, I must say it's the most hated travelling companion for a Cabin Crew member. Jet lag happens when you can't adjust your body clock to the local time, when there is a time difference from the place you left. At the Maldives, it gets completely dark at six in the afternoon, so it means if you are planning to get tan at the beach, you better set up your alarm early. I must say, I wasn't able to get out of bed before mid-day any day, because I was so bloody jet lagged. I would snooze my alarm every thirty minutes every morning, as I was so tired and sleepy. The whole jetlag thing was new to me, so I didn't know how to deal with it! And the consequence of getting up late every morning was, that I was going to bed late too.

Despite having to get up very early every day and I was living in a house with other Spanish guys, I can truly say, that those were happy times for me. Since my parents divorced in January of 1997, I didn't have the opportunity to live in a happy house. My parents were always fighting for custody of me and my sister and I was feeling like I was in the middle of a lost-battle. I guess that's why I have always wanted to live far away from home, as it could in a way, escape from all my miseries. After my parents got the divorce, my dad had the 'awesome' idea of moving to Dominican Republic. And deep inside me I knew that he would never come back. And he never did.

In England, I was on a temporary contract for the summer season only. Unfortunately, they did not renew my contract as Cabin Crew for the winter, so I had to go back to Barcelona. I found myself again, in the movie *Groundhog Day*. I was sleeping in my tiny bedroom at my parents' home, looking for another boring office job. As they say, misfortune never comes alone, so after a few months of being back home, we received the sad news that my father had passed away, so I was not really motivated to do anything during those times. However, I could say I was sure about something: I was still interested in going back to aviation and I was determined to be a long-haul Cabin Crew only, as I wanted to experience many layovers like the one, I had in the Maldives.

I quickly started to know which airlines were the best and worst to work at. The first time I heard about middle eastern airlines was when my flat mate John told me that he was going to attend an Open Day in London. At that time, only a few people knew about Dubai and these fantastic opportunities for Cabin Crew in the middle east, as there were not many direct flights in between Europe and the United Arab Emirates and Dubai was not a tourist destination yet. The middle eastern airlines were well-known amongst crew because of their competitive benefits and their cool destination map and layovers. But there was a 'small' inconvenient: if successful, you needed to move to Dubai which was in a Muslim country.

Unfortunately for John, he did not get the job; however, that did not stop him going to Dubai on vacation to visit his friend Paul. Paul was the only guy we knew, who had successfully passed the recruitment process for a middle-eastern airline.

3 EVERYTHING HAPPENS FOR A REASON

I will always remember the summer of 2007 as a magical one. Without knowing that it would be my last one in Spain for a long time. I spent that summer with my friends, travelling to cool beach destinations and enjoying it to the maximum. Thank god I did that as I don't recall having that kind of holiday in a long time! In one of the trips I did, I went to the island of Menorca to visit my friend David, who was there visiting his parents as he was also living in Barcelona. One night, David and his family were attending a private party in *Cova d'en Xoroi* club, however, because I didn't have an invitation and I didn't feel like going out, I decided to stay in and chill at their beautiful house. The truth was that I was broke and I also wanted to save some money, as I was unemployed at that moment.

Call it luck or fate, but the fact that I didn't go out that night was the consequence of what happened to me in the next eight years of my life. If you have watched the movie *The butterfly effect* you would be able to understand what I am talking about, which is just about how a simple event in a single moment of your life, can make the domino pieces fall all in a certain direction. And for me, that direction, was taking me to Dubai.

I drunk a couple of beers and I decided to log in to *Windows Messenger* (we didn't have *Facebook* at that time) to check who was online, so I could chat to someone, while I was waiting for David to come back from the club. Paul, the guy who was living in Dubai, was also online at that time. To be honest, he was one of these people who you have on your contact list, but you had never spoken to him before. But that night, I felt like it would be a good idea to introduce myself to him, as I was also curious about how life in Dubai would be. And he was hot too! After a few hours (and a few beers), Paul explained to me about how fantastic and fun it was to be a Cabin Crew member in Dubai. It looked like a dream: you would be flying all over the world and you would be getting paid for it. Once in the destination, you would be sleeping in five-star hotels and you would be getting an allowance on the layover, apart from your tax-free salary each month! And on top of that, you would be living in a complimentary fully furnished bedroom apartment with all the utilities included too! Paul also told me that there was swimming pool and gym in each crew's accommodation where you could relax on your days off, since the temperature was always nice and warm in Dubai.

It was all about the luxe life they were living (his flat mate had just bought a Hummer!) and how their financial situation had improved since they were living there. And on top of that, they'd been all over the world already. It seemed unreal to me!

"Come on, Carmen! You should come to Dubai to visit me like John and Frank did! And then Peter can take us around in his Hummer!" Paul suggested while sipping from his can of beer.

"I'm not sure, I don't have any money… but where do I stay anyway? I don't even know you in person!" I replied laughing while thinking about the exotic idea of being in a hummer with such a good looking and friendly guy.

"Don't worry about it, you can stay in our apartment, it's always full of people anyway, and I can tell the security guys downstairs that you are my cousin! I just need to fill the visitors form and *khalas*! And you can even stay for a month, it will be fun!" Paul said to me as he lit another cigarrete. Apparently, you could not have any female friends staying at your apartment if you were a male and vice versa, so everyone would use the word 'cousin' when having a visitor from the opposite gender.

"Paul, if I go to Dubai it's going to be as a Flight Attendant too!" I said back to him while seeing through the camera that there were in fact lots of people in his apartment, especially lots of pretty girls.

"Look, this is simple: if you like travelling, meeting new people and partying, this is the place to be!"

This was the kind of life I've always wanted to have and the one I had always dreamed of. And that seemed much better than the life of my friend Mary! It was the right moment for me to go as I was unemployed, and I didn't have anything to lose but a lot to win. After our video call, I started surfing online about the airline and the famous 'Open Days' held all over the world. Apparently, it was very difficult to get through the recruitment process. Anyway. One thing I did remember about John's Open Day last year in London is, that they were coming to Spain twice a year, but I wasn't sure if they had been already that year.

While the careers website was opening, I suddenly felt the need to participate. My surprise was, that the next Open Day in Barcelona would be taking place in two weeks! I couldn't believe how lucky I was, and I started to believe that this could only be a sign. As I only had two weeks to organize myself, I started reading everything I could on the internet about Dubai and the airline I was dreaming to work for, and I thoroughly prepared for my big day.

4 THE INTERVIEW

The 23rd of August 2007 my life took a hundred- and eighty-degree turn. David and I decided to attend the Open Day in Barcelona, so we shared a taxi and we headed to the hotel where the recruitment process was taking place. We were both very nervous, but unlike David, you could not tell I was nervous. I woke up feeling happy and confident as deep inside me because I knew that Dubai was waiting for me.

When we arrived at the hotel where the Open Day was taking place, we noticed that there were lots of people in suits and impeccable grooming and they were all holding a curriculum vitae in their hands. Despite it being summer time and mostly everyone was on holidays, there were around a hundred applicants there. If you were lucky enough to be successful throughout the day, the recruitment process usually would last for two to three days, as it would consist of four or five round of eliminatory stages, where candidates would be assessed in different areas. The face to face interview being the last step. But if you weren't lucky enough, you could be sent home after the CV drop off.

The day went by and I was passing all tests. The group became much smaller, and after each round, I would call my mum to tell her that I was getting through the process. My mum was not happy about the idea of me moving that far away and in a Muslim country. However, she was slowly accepting the idea, as she saw that I was getting through the day. I became one of the final candidates and I was invited to the face to face interview the following day. My friends John and Frank from London were waiting for me at Barcelona's beach as they thought that I would leave soon. The only guy that we knew that got through the process was our friend Paul and he was like the perfect guy: charming and good looking. So, they did not believe what was happening to me.

"Carmen, you're going to live in Dubai with Paul!"- John said to me.

"Hmmm, I'm not sure, I hope so! Do you really think so?"

"You will see. As someone I know told me once, everything happens for a reason"- And I knew he was referring to me   back in London, I would use this quote a lot.

Six weeks after the interview at six in the morning, I received the famous golden call, congratulating me and telling that I had been selected for the job and my joining flight to go to Dubai would be in a month's time. I could not believe it! I thanked the universe for giving me this life changing opportunity and deep inside me I knew, that my life was about to change forever.

5 MOVING TO DUBAI

The on boarding process to join the airline was a bit of a nightmare when it comes to paperwork, as the job offer was conditioned to a successful medical examination before moving to Dubai. They wanted to check if we had any pre-existing medical conditions and if we were in excellent health conditions to do the job. Luckily, I was good to go!

After weeks of farewell parties and the pressure of packing only a suitcase for my brand-new life in the Middle East, the day that I was leaving Barcelona arrived. I was going to live in a Muslim country at the other side of the world, and I pretty much didn't know where I was going to live, who I would be sharing the apartment with or if I would like to live there. The only person I knew from Dubai was Paul, but I hadn't spoken to him again since our video call in summer. I also didn't know, If I would be able to cope with the fact of living in a Muslim country, far from everyone. But still, I was thankful for the opportunity I had been given of starting a new life from scratch. My original idea was, to go to Dubai for a year only, unless I liked it there, so I would then finish the three-year contract I had signed for. But I must admit… if someone had told me back then, that I would be living in Dubai for eight years… I would not have believed it!

On my adjoining flight to Dubai, I was observing the crew and the aircraft, as I knew that this was going to be 'my office' for the next few years. They all looked very nice and well groomed. Once we landed at the Dubai International Airport, we had to look for the *Marhaba* team which, I knew years later, that *Marhaba* means welcome in Arabic.

While walking through the airport and looking for the *Marhaba* team, I noticed a couple of guys carrying very heavy suitcases, and they looked like they were looking for someone too. And, like me, you could see from their faces that they had a mixture of excitement and wonder.

"Good morning ma'am! Good morning sir! This way please! Welcome to Dubai!" The two Pilipino ladies from the *Marhaba* team seemed lovely and they looked like they would be singing instead of talking to us.

Once we were all there, they escorted us to the bus that would take us to our designated apartments. Paul had advised me that some crew buildings had better location than others, so you could be lucky to be at the largest road of Dubai full of lights tall buildings, restaurants and shops, or you could be in a less fancy area, which was closer to the airport though. I was praying to be in the good one!

Inside the bus, I saw that the area that we were passing through was indeed the less fancy one, as I couldn't see any sky buildings and I saw lots of mosques instead. The bus would stop when it arrived at any of the crew accommodations that had been assigned to us. Back at the airport, the Marhaba team had given us a card with a building name written in it. I was meant to be at the *Gold building*. It was the first time I had been in a Muslim country. And to be honest, I knew very little about their religion and traditions. The only thing I knew was, that we had to dress in a more conservative way than we would do at home and kissing in public was not allowed. I also knew that during a period of time called *Ramadan*, Muslims would fast and sleep during the day, as I remembered from my Pakistani ex work colleagues in London.

I didn't get the feeling that I was in Dubai, until we entered Sheikh Zayed road, which was named after the first president of the United Arab Emirates in 1971. *Sheikh Zayed Road* was the most important and spectacular road at that time, and it connects Dubai with Abu Dhabi (UAE's capital) and *Ras al Khaimah*. I felt like I was in New York but with the exception that all the signs were in Arabic, which I found quite funny actually!

Back in 2007, Dubai was very different city from how it is now. Dubai was not even considered a tourist destination, and half of the most iconic buildings like *Burj Khalifa* or Atlantis, were not even built yet. There was no subway yet and the Dubai international airport as we know it now, didn't exist. At that time, *Burj Khalifa* was still half-way built and it didn't even have a name yet. I will tell you an anecdote about it, as when the global economic recession hit Dubai in 2009, the building's construction was stopped because there was not enough funding. The ruler of Abu Dhabi, *His Highness Sheikh Khalifa bin Zayed Al Nahyan*, volunteered to pay for the building to be finished, with the condition of naming the building after his name. So, now you know where Khalifa comes from and Burj means tower in Arabic.

Its diverse and fast-growing economy has led to incredible growth through the decades. In 2016, the population of Dubai was over two million and a half, and the city was expected to see continued steady growth in the years ahead. With just only fifteen per cent of the population composed by local Emirati residents, the remaining eighty-five per cent are expatriates. More commonly referred to as expats, are foreigners that move to Dubai, often lured by the promise of excellent salaries and luxury living.

In the city of Dubai more than hundred and forty nationalities live together in harmony. Thanks to all the international residents in Dubai, the city has demonstrated to excel in mixing influences from many countries. For example, in Dubai you could find British traditions such as going for brunch or to horse racing, Muslim traditions like *Eid* or *Ramadan*, or the Hindu *Holi Festival of Colours*. Even a Christian festivity like Christmas, it's also celebrated in Dubai. It's incredible how much a city can change and develop in a short period of time, considering that it wasn't that long ago when the city was only about camels and dhows, as it was a small fishing settlement for pearl traders. However, everything changed for Dubai with the discovery of oil in 1960s, bringing a soaring business and an army of traders who flocked to the emirate to settle there.

"We arrived Gold building, please!" The bus driver yelled at us in a very strong Indian accent that I could barely understand.

"Excuse me sir, have you just said Gold Building?"

"Gold building". He repeated and seemed a bit annoyed by my question. "That's me, thank you very much sir". I said while I was visually checking that I was not forgetting anything inside the bus.

I pointed out my baggage to the bus driver and I thanked him for the ride. I wasn't sure if I had to tip him, but I didn't have any dirhams yet. Luckily for me, my apartment was located at *Sheikh Zayed road*, just in front of the future *Burj Khalifa* building and the future Dubai mall. It was almost two in the morning when I entered the massive and beautiful apartment that from this moment on, would be my home. I went outside of my bedroom's balcony and I lit a cigarette, while I looked at the busy road full of lights, I thought about how long I would end up living here.

6 THE GLAMOROUS LIFE OF A FLIGHT ATTENDANT

I don't know what it is, but pretty much everyone thinks that the Cabin Crew job is a very cool job: you get to travel around the world, and you get paid for it. And if on top of that, you get free accommodation in the opulent city of Dubai, you end up being the most envied person of your friends back home.

The Cabin Crew training lasted for six weeks and they trained us in subjects like first aid, safety, security and service. I had previously flown as a Flight Attendant in England, but this was a completely new experience. Unlike other airlines, we also got trained in how to serve different passengers according to their cultural background, how we should take care of our health and diet, or how-to put-on our makeup according to their strict grooming standards. After we successfully completed our training, we got our first monthly flight rosters. We were so excited thinking where in the world we would be flying first.

"Where are you going on your *suppy* flight, Carmen?" Jessica asked me while trying to have a sneaky look at my flight sheet. A supernumerary flight (*suppy* flight) is a familiarisation flight where you don't get a position on board and you are mainly there to observe in preparation for your first operational flight, so you would get involved in all aspects of the service, the cabin and the galley.

"Oh no! Can you believe that my first flight ever is to 'lovely' Birmingham, in the UK? Like there are no other places in the world for me to go!" I didn't know if I should laugh or cry as I couldn't believe how unlucky I was. "How about you, where are you going, Jess?"

"I am going to Bangkok! I heard that massages are awesome there and everything is so cheap! Can't wait!". Jess was over the moon with her flight.

"I bet you can't!" I replied to her while I was trying to figure out if I had also been rostered with any of the cool trips.

Jess was from Mexico and she became one of my best friends in Dubai. She would always be making fun of everything and she would have this weird Mexican vocabulary that would make me laugh. I would love being at her place all the time, even though she was living at the less fancy area of Dubai and her food specialty at that time would be noodle soup in a cup with some cheese on the top. The good thing about flying long haul and short haul was, that you were getting the chance to fly to new and exciting places, and you were also getting the chance to have short turnarounds in case you wanted to be in Dubai with your friends. Jess and I used to call each other right after a flight and even from the aircraft still, if we knew that we were both in town.

I remember my first months as Cabin Crew as a bit crazy, as every day was a new adventure where you'd meet new people and see a new country pretty much every day of work. It didn't matter if you had a six-hour flight to Rome, a twelve-hour flight to New York or a very early morning flight from Glasgow, because there was no excuse: you had to meet at the lobby right after the flight, to visit the city and have a few drinks with the rest of the crew. Since I am an extroverted person, I like socializing and being around people all the time. That's why I had so much fun at the beginning, as it was rare that I would feel lonely. Also, if you did make friends on the flight, you would also be meeting for a few drinks right after landing in Dubai. Long haul flying was fun but exhausting, as you would never be catching up on sleep. However, I was still young, and it didn't really matter to me at that time if sometimes I was going on a flight without properly sleeping enough, as it was always hard to adjust the body clock once in Dubai after flying to far destinations all the time. And Dubai was a very amusing city to live in, as every day of the week there were unlimited things to do and events to attend.

During my first year, I had travelled more than what a wealthy family would have travelled in their whole life. I had walked on the *Great Wall of China*, I had swum in the crystal waters of Mauritius island or Seychelles, I had hugged a koala in Australia, I had taken a picture with a Japanese *Geisha* and I had ridden an elephant in Sri Lanka. However, if you paid attention to the crew, you could see the different energy levels amongst Cabin Crew and that would vary according to their joining date, the cabin that they were working at, and their uniform size!

In economy cabin, everyone was always up to anything: sightseeing, shopping, dinner… They were even happy to go for dinner even when the captain would suggest it! (Note: nobody likes to hang out with the pilots because they are boring!). Cabin crew in economy were mostly young, single and slim. Once you would become a business class crew, your energy levels would drop substantially as you would start feeling very tired. Plus, as business class crew, you would have already done all the cool flights to new destinations. So, after the exhausting long haul flights that they would have to operate on with a higher level of service excellence, (customers pay more in business so they are more demanding), they would prefer to rest in the layover, or they would just go shopping to buy this special thing that you would only get in that specific country. Like for example, *Victoria's Secret* or *Bath and Body Works* in the United States.

Business class crew also preferred to hang out at the lobby bar, so after a couple of drinks, they could go straight to their rooms to rest. With regards to their personal life, most of them would be dating someone or engaged already, as they have been living in Dubai for at least a couple of years already. And what can I say about First Class cabin crew … They were the ones that would get paid more and would work less. They were also the ones that would eat better on board, since they have the first-class passengers. First class crew were usually always tired and depressed about the job itself and about their life in Dubai. Once they reached the layover, they would go straight to the hotel rooms avoiding any contact with the crew.

Unfortunately, the more you would stay in this job and the older you would get, the unhappier you would be, as the majority didn't know how to leave this easy but exhausting life full of nothing but air. On top of that, some crew were also feeling trapped with the job and with Dubai, as most of them had loans or mortgages to pay, or families that they were supporting financially back home… However, you don't really understand their behaviour and what they are going through, until you become one of them.

I can assure you that what they say about the crew makes the flight, it's so true. Having nice destinations in the roster would not guarantee the fact that you would have fun. As we were a different set of crews in each flight, it was difficult to predict if it will be a fun or a boring trip, as it mostly depended on the crew that would operate the flight with you, as well as the type of passengers that you could have. A very important part was also depending on the flight supervisors, as they could be hardworking people who led by example, or they could be mean to crew and have an attitude of reporting everything to the office. For instance, a seven-day trip to Australia that initially would be very exciting on your flight roster, it could be the worst nightmare if no one from the crew wanted to hang out or do anything during the layover, because that meant that you would spend a week all by yourself and with serious jetlag.

It is true that sometimes you need a full day to yourself in order to do your stuff, but the truth is, that a full week with no one to speak to might be too depressing, or at least it was for me. On the other hand, sometimes a less popular and exciting layover, could be the best trip ever if the crew was nice.

7 TIME FLIES WHEN YOU ARE HAVING FUN

The years were passing by quickly at the blink of an eye. Since my sickness ratio was very low, I quickly got promoted to business class cabin and after two and a half years of flying for the airline, I got the opportunity to become cabin supervisor. I was thankful to the airline and I felt recognized, because I was given the opportunity to learn about managing teams as well as the opportunity to gain leadership skills, so I couldn't complain.

I have a lot of good memories of my years as Flight Attendant. We worked hard, however we were also trying to have fun as well. As you can imagine, I have a hundred stories to tell which would give me content to write another book. But It wouldn't be fair, not to share any of these fun or awkward moments that I experienced on board, with you. I will never forget the flight from Kuwait to Dubai that I operated once, during Ramadan. For those who don't know, Ramadan is that time of the year where Muslims fast from dawn until sunset, and they refrain from consuming food, drinking liquids, smoking, and engaging in sexual relations. Usually, the type of passengers that would travel on that flight, would be either business men or local people from the UAE or Kuwait.

There was an Arab couple seated in business class and they were both wearing the traditional Gulf clothing. When it comes to the Gulf, it's easy to spot its citizens, as they have kept wearing their traditional clothes since they were Bedouins. Men in the Gulf usually wear a long, white tunic called dishdasha, and this tunic is usually worn with short *sherwal* trousers and a *ghutra*, white headscarf. Women wear wide, long robes called *abayas*, usually in association with a *hijab* that shows some hair and a *niqab*. So, by the look of their clothes and since we were at 'that time of the year', I expected them to be behaving as any Muslim would do in such a spiritual time like Ramadan.

Right after the *Iftar* service, (evening meal where Muslims break their daily Ramadan fast) the Arab gentlemen came to the galley and asked us for a glass of red wine. He drank it very fast and he was making sure that no one could see him. After a few minutes, the Arab guy came to the galley again and asked us for another glass of red wine. He drank it even faster, as if it was a tequila shot and went back to his seat again. My surprise was that after a few minutes, he came back and asked us for one last glass of red wine. I was shocked and confused, as I saw that he was getting drunk and I knew that in Islam, consumption of alcoholic beverages is generally forbidden in the *Qur'an*. I couldn't deny serving him alcohol, as you could get fired if a customer complained about you, and if that customer was a local Emirati or Kuwaiti, even worse. I also noticed that he was hiding from his wife, as he wasn't drinking the wine at his seat.

"Mr. Hussein, I don't mind giving you another glass of wine to you again, but... don't you think that your wife will find out that you have been drinking?" I told him in the politest way possible, so I wouldn't be in trouble.

"Don't worry, my wife has no idea what the smell of wine is". He said to me with a big and naughty smile on his face.

And I smiled back, thinking what a fraud he was. I think this is a great example that summarizes the hypocrisy of Dubai.

UAE is under *Shariah* law, therefore people who consume or possess alcohol must have a liquor permit or they may face arrest, fines and possible imprisonment. Alcohol is served in most hotels in Dubai, but technically that's only for hotel guests. On top of that, liquor licenses are only issued to people who possess current UAE residency permit and who are non-Muslim. So, if you are Muslim and if you get caught for being intoxicated, the penalty is even more severe, as it also includes corporal punishment.

In a more positive note, I also remember those flights when Muslim pilgrims from around the world would travel to Mecca (Saudi Arabia) to perform the *Hajj*. It's interesting how a journey that once took months on camelback can now be completed within hours by plane! *Hajj* brings together Muslims from all over the world, regardless of culture, ethnicity or class. In the *Qur'an* it says, that it's a religious duty that Muslims should perform at least once in their lives.

The funny thing is, that on those *Hajj* flights, pilgrims would board the aircraft in big groups wearing anything but white towels around their waists and shoulders. I can assure you that the first time that you operate one of those flights from Dubai to Jeddah is quite impressive, as all these passengers from different nationalities are dressed like if they were going to a jacuzzi! There is a reason behind everybody wearing the same type of white cloth and is because it prevents people from judging each other's wealth or status, symbolizing also the equality of every Muslim before God.

Chinese flights were also quite unusual, especially when after taking off, all Chinese passengers would remove their shoes and change into hotel slippers. By looking at their feet, it was easy to spot in which hotel they had stayed in: *Marriot, Shangri-La, Le Meridien,* and some of the Chinese passengers were stretching at the back of the aircraft like if they were in a Yoga or Taiichi class. But the worst thing wasn't the fact that it looked like a spa, it was the terrible smell of feet that the whole cabin had!

African flights were always very busy and the aircrafts that the airline would use for those type of flights would be the elder ones from the fleet. Therefore, the flights were not as comfortable and because they were quite old, passengers would always have issues with broken seats or the inflight entertainment system not operative. However, African passengers would never complain about anything but food, as they were never satisfied with just one meal! On those flights, you would always run out of meals, drinks and duty-free items. They would grab your arm and they would tell you: "give me food, I'm hungry". Apart from the food issue, passengers would be super nice and friendly on the flight.

One of the less popular trips that none of the crew wanted to operate was Lagos, in Nigeria. Lagos was the only layover from the whole airline network where our crew bus was escorted by heavily armed police, because the city is dangerous, and crime is an ongoing problem. There was once a rumour of an airline crew that was kidnapped and killed on their way from the airport to the hotel in Nigeria, but I've never found out if the story was true, or just another gossip. On a more positive note I must say that allowance in Lagos was one of the highest that we would get for a twenty-four-hour layover (around hundred and sixty US dollars) and you were safe if you didn't step outside of the hotel.

Indian flights were the busiest and more demanding flights above all. And because of that, those flights were also the ones with the highest ratio of crew calling sick and crew not showing up to the flight. As crew, you would get at least three to four Indian turnarounds a month. The thing about those flights were that they were all departing from Dubai around three in the morning (crew reporting time was always three hours before the flight), and they would be landing back in Dubai around two in the afternoon if they weren't any delays. Those flights would be a killer for everyone, because even if you were lucky to take a three-hour nap in the afternoon, you would be knackered.

8 THE 'NOT SO GLAMOROUS' PART OF THE JOB

Flying for one of the world's best airlines gave me the opportunity to visit many countries that I would have never visited if I wouldn't have had the opportunity to fly for a middle eastern airline. I was getting a tax-free salary and free accommodation in Dubai and I didn't have to worry about paying bills or how I would get to the end of the month. I was sightseeing, shopping, partying and sleeping in five-star hotels all over the world and I was getting paid for that! I was certainly getting used to a life full of little luxuries, which were already becoming my day to day. But the hidden reality of this 'glamorous life' was that it wasn't glamorous at all.

It didn't take me long until I found out that the job of a Flight Attendant was physically very exhausting due to long hours of work, endless services on board and due to crossing several time zones in a day. Behind that mandatory red lipstick that female crew had to wear, there was a hidden reality that the airline management was trying to ignore by punishing the crew if they would call in sick or if they would underperform on board, according to their strict service standards. Although we had free housing and free transportation to go to work, we were lacking the main conditions that any other airline would offer like proper rest periods, a full company paid health insurance, and a guaranteed non-flying position during pregnancy. The main issue was that labour disputes and unions, common elsewhere in the airline industry, were banned in the UAE so we could not fight for our rights as employees.

What they didn't tell us when we signed our initial three-year contract to join the airline was that we couldn't get pregnant because we would get fired. And if we got pregnant without being married, we would go to prison for having sex outside marriage. Unfortunately, I have witnessed a few stories of Cabin Crew having to go through abortion outside of the UAE or having to deliver a baby in the bathroom floor of a hotel room in a layover, so they would avoid jail. In Europe, pregnant women are protected from being fired as most airlines find their staff work on ground or place them on maternity leave. If you would fall pregnant during your first three-year contract even though you were married, work conditions weren't good either, since you wouldn't have pregnancy medical coverage and you would have to stop working from the very first month. They would remove your identification card, your flying benefits (so you could not travel back home to have a doctor monitoring your pregnancy) and your housing allowance and medical expenses would be at your own cost.

As crew, our rosters were composed mainly by night turnarounds and long-haul flights. We were operating fourteen-hour flights from Dubai to all continents and we would cross quite a few time zones in each flight. The effects of time zone changes were usually more noticeable on the longer flights and many summed it up simply as 'jet lag'. However, frequent flying over more than three time zones can throw one's circadian rhythm (twenty-four-hour cycle in the physiological processes of living beings) out of sync. Once the body clock is out of sync, you would start experiencing sleep disturbance, difficulty in concentration, confusion and irritability, just to name a few. It wasn't long after I started having sleeping problems as I was suffering from jet lag in the layovers and in Dubai. At the beginning, I didn't think that it was a big deal not having any rest before my flights, as apparently everyone was going through the same thing. Therefore, when everyone is in the same boat as you, you start normalizing the outrageous. In the galley talks after the on-board service, one of the most popular topics was to talk about which pills we could use in Dubai if we wanted to fall asleep quickly, since we had a long list of banned medications that were prohibited to bring or use in the UAE and they were also prohibited by the airline.

In my first few years as Cabin Crew, I was surviving on the flights thanks to sleep-inducing pills that most of us would take. We weren't fully sure if we would be allowed to use them or not, or if they would result positive in the event of a random drug test. The only thing that we cared was the fact that we didn't need a prescription to get them. It was common to get to a hotel room after a sixteen-hour flight without being able to have any sleep. It is an indescribable feeling when you are dead tired, and you close your eyes, but still, you can't sleep.

It wasn't well seen at the airline if a crew member called sick quite often to their flights, as this would cause serious consequences on their job promotions and salary. Therefore, it resulted in crew avoiding calling in sick to their flights even if they were unfit to fly to avoid penalties. Crew were showing serious fatigue symptoms on board which was even worse. For instance, if a Flight Attendant would close their eyes in the jump seat during descent and in front of passengers, it was reported to the office and heavily punished with downgrades or final warnings. And if you as Supervisor would not report the issue, you would be punished as well if they found out. Obviously if the crew was not well rested, it was a safety issue as our primary responsibility on board was to guard everyone's safety.

And on top of all these challenges on board, you had the passengers. Most of our passengers knew that by complaining they would get things for free. The airline management would take any of these passenger complaints in a very serious way and they would always be on the customer side as the old saying goes customers are always right. Therefore, having a passenger complaining about you, could cost you the job. Even myself I have almost lost my job during my first year of flying when a customer got seriously angry at me because he didn't get his meal choice. After I apologized and explained to the customer that there was no chicken left in the entire aircraft as we weren't in a restaurant, the passenger started threatening me by saying that he was friends with the *Sheikh* of Dubai (although he was seated at the last of economy class!). When my Supervisor was informed about the issue, she told me that she had to report that incident to the office. Finally, after crying and begging her not to do so, she decided not to mention it in our flight performance appraisal. Otherwise, I would have not be able to have written this book as my flying career in the middle east would have stopped not long after.

As a result of the above, most of the crew feared losing their jobs and a few of them would even have depression. It would depend on every person's resilience to the challenges of the job. Perhaps some of you might think that the easiest solution would have been to leave the job, but we really don't know each person's personal situation. Maybe that Flight Attendant was feeding the whole family back home and they were all dependent on his or her salary, or maybe their country was at war... Or maybe that person was stuck in Dubai for another thirty years because of a mortgage. Therefore, a constant fear mentality was always present in the back of our mind that if we did something wrong, we would be sent back home, or we would even be sent to prison.

9 LIFE IN DUBAI

Your life in Dubai was really depending on how flexible and open minded you would be with the downsides of living in a Muslim country and with the many rules you had to adhere to because of the *Shariah* law. It was a great city to live in, however it wasn't for everyone. Dubai could be the most spectacular life experience you would ever have but it could also be the worst living nightmare. Being surrounded by good friends was also key, considering most of us didn't move to Dubai with our families, so when living thousand miles away, your best friends become your family. However, even if you had friends and acquaintances in Dubai, it was unavoidable to feel lonely since a lot of times it was difficult for everyone to be in Dubai at the same time. I remember that my worst fear was to end up alone on Christmas or New Year's Eve.

It almost happened to me on my first Christmas in Dubai as I had only been there for six weeks, and the only people I knew seemed to have exciting plans of family visiting or awesome trips on their flight roster. So, I had two options: to spend the night on the computer chatting with my family and let them know how miserable I was feeling, or contact everyone I had met during the past weeks and check if there were any Christmas gatherings going on... I decided to go for the second one, however I felt weird going to someone's place where I barely knew anyone. Would I have done this if it happened to me in Barcelona? Of course not, but I guess I would have never experienced a situation like that if I was back home. But in Dubai, most of the times we had to get out of our comfort zone if you wanted to get things done.

Living in Dubai was everything but normal. One of the things that shocked me the most was when I found out that the weekdays would go from Sunday to Thursday. Friday was the day of congregation, which meant that all Muslims needed to go to the mosque to pray. Congregational prayers (obligatory for men) are one of the most strongly emphasized duties in Islam. It is a time when Muslims come together to pray in order to reaffirm their faith and devotion to *Allah*. Basically, every mosque in Dubai would have a speaker so you could hear the prayer everywhere 'live', even if the speaker man would be coughing. So, the noon prayer on Friday was the time and day for the congregational prayer, and the time and day where you should avoid trying to get a taxi or even going to the supermarket as the whole city would be on standby until they returned from the mosque.

Another quite interesting thing about Dubai was when I found out that streets had no names. Just a couple of streets like *Sheikh Zayed Road* or Jumeirah road had a name and instead they would use landmarks for directions, like for example hotels or touristic attractions. The real challenge was, when we were new in Dubai and we would take a taxi with a Pakistani driver who would also be new, and he wouldn't have any clue where the Ramada hotel was. However, we would still pretend to know where we were going, so drivers would not take advantage of us, in case they weren't the new guy in town at all.

As I previously mentioned, local Emiratis would still wear their traditional clothes, so it was easy to spot them. The same thing would happen with Indians, as some of them would wear the traditional Indian *saree*. For us expats, we always had to be mindful of our way of dressing. We all knew that we had to dress in a conservative and respectful way, however we could dress in a more relaxed way if we were going straight to the beach.

In every shopping mall and restaurant, there was a poster reminding you about how you should behave and dress in public. No kissing was allowed, holding hands was not allowed either, and wearing shorts was not allowed. I remember once I got a verbal warning from a security guy in the Mall of Emirates because I kissed my boyfriend at that time in public! I don't think I have ever been so embarrassed in my whole life! Oh yes, hang on, I had another experience an even worse one… In one of those really hot summer days where the temperature was above fifty degrees Celsius, I went to buy some groceries at the supermarket behind my building. I was wearing flip flops and a pair of shorts (note: they weren't the type of shorts where you could see half of the ass, as they were not sexy at all!), so the superstore security guard stopped me without letting me in. I was so embarrassed as when these things happen everyone starts looking at you (and your shorts). I had already been living in Dubai for more than five years and I was going there quite often, so I felt offended as they had treated me like If I was another tourist.

You really needed to have a good sense of humour and take your life as easy as you could, as Dubai was a proper tourist attraction without even going sightseeing. It wasn't strange to find fast food restaurants where they would serve camel meat and camel milk, ATM machines where you could take out golden bars, or local Emiratis driving Lamborghinis with a panther as co-pilot.

Whereas expats and local Emiratis would be living in the same city, we would rarely mix. Even considering that we would shop in the same malls, we would go to the same restaurants and we would watch movies at the same movie theatre. Emiratis are well known as friendly people, but truth is, unless you would share workplace or your kids would go to the same school, you would not interact with them most likely because of the cultural gap. Immigrant construction workers would not be considered as part of the expat community- although construction workers and expatriates are both migrants- connotations in Dubai would be very different: expats were described as educated, rich and professionals working abroad, while those less privileged were deemed foreign workers or migrant workers.

Dubai is a melting pot of culture; the perfect blend between modernity and tradition, the old and the new and so were the local Emiratis and the expats. We were all part of this place and ultimately, we would all contribute to its uniqueness. So, in many ways, many expats would be just as much a local as Emiratis, since in a way, we have all helped to build the sand pit as we know it now.

10 HANGING UP THE WINGS

When I reached my fifth-year flying, I started considering hanging up my wings for good. That expression in aeronautical jargon means when you decide to stop flying. I had reached the point where I was feeling very tired and I was not enjoying the job anymore. Instead of hanging out with the crew or going sightseeing whenever I had a trip, I would watch television in my hotel bedroom in the layovers. I was operating the flights like if I was a robot and the galley chats with my twenty-year-old crew became boring to me, as they would always be talking about the same topics: boyfriends, travel destinations, parties in Dubai, complaints about the airline… Service standards became stricter every day and my role as flight supervisor did not satisfy me anymore. It was the time to find a real job. Flying the world had been a fun and great experience, however I didn't see myself doing it forever. I wanted to find another kind of job, but I was not sure what I would do or where I would do it.

The economic situation in Spain wasn't good because the country was still recovering from the financial crisis, so the option of going back home was not on the cards. Plus, I didn't have anywhere to stay other than my mum's house and after living by myself for so long, it would be hard for me to return in that way. I didn't know what opportunities would be available for me with five years flying experience. I knew from other colleagues, that it was quite difficult to find a job because companies outside aviation industry didn't understand how our experience on board could apply to their businesses. As Cabin Crew, we were given the opportunity to learn valuable soft skills on board, however, we were lacking experience in an office environment and solid computer skills, that at the end of the day, it was the most important thing to work for a company. Most of the crew had had ground jobs before starting their flying career and most of them had studied at university before joining the airline, too. Therefore, those who

27

wanted to go back to normal life, would rely on that previous experience on ground when looking for a job. During my last two years of flying, I did benefit from my free time during my layovers, and I studied an online post-graduate degree in Marketing Management.

My initial idea was to work for the airline's communication department, but I had only found a temporary job so there was no point in resigning from my permanent cabin crew job. I created the habit of looking at internal vacancies in order to see if there was anything I could fit in, according to my profile but I didn't find anything that interested me until I saw a job posting that attracted my attention: Cabin Crew Recruitment Officer! I remembered how great my Recruiters were during my Open Day and I thought that it could be a very interesting and rewarding job I could do as it was to recruit new cabin crew members into the airline. So, I read the job requirements and without any hesitation, I decided to apply for the job.

I didn't want to tell anyone about my idea of hanging up the wings because I didn't want anyone to influence my decision, so I preferred to keep the secret for myself. Moving to a new role on ground would represent a big change in my life, as well as a significant salary drop. However, I thought that would be a big stepping stone in my professional career, and the opportunity to learn about the HR function. I decided that I would speak with my Cabin Crew Manager to get more information about the role and guidance about the recruitment process since I knew that she had been supporting a few Cabin Crew Open Days in the past.

"Good morning Jane, thanks for chatting to me. As I explained to you earlier through email, I would like to apply to the cabin crew recruitment position that is currently advertised internally. I am very excited about it and I think I have the correct skill set and motivation to do this job. I thought that you could perhaps give me some inside information about the department and the role, to help me with my application, please?" I told my Manager in a very polite and professional manner.

"Oh, really? That's a shame if we lose you on board! Feedback from the pursers has been very positive, so we believe that with your current performance score, you wouldn't have to wait too long to become a Purser, will you?" My Manager said to me with in a casual Aussie accent and a big fake smile.

"Yes, I understand and thank you for that… but now that I have been flying for almost five years, I feel like I am ready for a new challenge within the airline… "I said to her while I started realising that she would not be willing to help me.

"Carmen... I am so sorry for this but this position in recruitment is quite popular amongst crew... more than four hundred applicants have already applied so, chances are extremely low to be successful in this one..." And I guess she realised from the sad look on my face that I was feeling so demotivated, so she changed her speech and her tone. "Don't get me wrong Carmen, but looking at your profile... I truly believe that you should start preparing for the next Purser's opening because I am sure that you would be great at it! Plus, Cabin Crew Recruiters have a much lower pay!!". A Purser is the person in charge of the cabin crew team on board.

Meeting with my Manager ended up being very discouraging. In another words, I got the feeling that she though I wasn't good enough for the role. I thanked her for the information, and I left thinking about everything that she said to me and the light I was seeing at the end of the tunnel started fading. That day I felt awful. The only person, who was supposed to help motivate and advise me on how to keep growing professionally within the airline, shattered my dream in the blink of an eye.

It's funny because that conversation with my Manager gave me the strength to prove her wrong. I was not going to allow anyone to destroy my dreams, so I started preparing myself for the selection process, and I started compiling all the possible information that could help me at the selection process of the recruiter role. Thanks to how well prepared I was and my positive energy, I finally got the job! I could not believe it! I was going to be one of the recruiters who would help fulfil the dreams of thousands of people around the world. And this is how I went from hanging up the wings to recruiting Cabin Crew for one of the best airlines in the world.

11 THANK YOU, NEXT

The life of a Cabin Crew Recruiter was just as exciting or even more than the life of a Flight Attendant. We would be still be travelling a lot, but instead of working on board, we would be working once we had reached the destination. So, if we were having an Open Day scheduled at a specific city, we would be travelling as passengers in business class the day before the recruitment session. The job itself was much more rewarding than the one as Cabin Crew, because at the end of the day your role was to 'give jobs' to people. Most of the time I felt like Santa Claus, as I was helping Cabin Crew wannabes achieve their dreams, by giving out the opportunity to get a better life.

We would be assigned around three recruitment events a month and we would stay around five nights in each city where the Open Day was held. For example, in a month, you could be sent to two different cities in Italy for ten days, and a five-day trip to Boston. Our Team Leader Monica would send us to our countries of origin quite regularly, because she believed that there was no one better than ourselves that could understand our own people and culture. And she was right. By sending us home that often, she would also keep us motivated to do our jobs better, which was very nice of her and I personally think, that it was a great formula.

Since I am Spanish, I was spending around ten days a month in Spanish cities that I hadn't even been to before, so that was awesome! Having the opportunity to visit your closest ones every two months was better than salary raises. Plus, by living half of the month in five-star hotels all around the world I was not spending any money from my basic salary. Although my current salary was lower than when I was crew, I had the feeling that I was not spending anything when being away from Dubai, because Dubai was quite expensive and the more social life you had, the more you would spend.

Just a couple of months after I joined the cabin crew recruitment team and in order to save costs, the management team decided to reduce the number of two Recruiters to just one, in those cities where we usually had less than two hundred and fifty applicants attending. Luckily for me, I was still learning from the most experience ones, so during my first six months of employment I would always be accompanied by a senior Recruiter. They wouldn't be happy with the new procedures in place, complaining about how overloaded they would be and how lonely they would feel as they would have no one to speak to other than the candidates, for fifteen days a month.

Even though my job was to give jobs, the whole world was struggling to get out of a deep economic crisis. Most of the candidates from first world countries were attending to our global Open Days, dreaming with the opportunity to travel the world and live their first experience away from home, like if was a proper adventure. But there were many other candidates from a more disadvantaged countries, who would see the job as an opportunity to financially support their families.

It was heart-breaking when we had to reject candidates because they were not ticking all the boxes with the strict physical qualities checklist that we had to apply on each candidate. Especially, when they would tell us that they had travelled five hundred kilometres by coach from their village in order to attend the Open Day, or they had spent all their savings on the bus ticket. It was also heart-breaking when we were rejecting a candidate, because her ears were too pointy, or her teeth were too yellow, according to the strict airline standards. If they were unlucky enough to have a bad complexion, weight problems, visible scars or tattoos, most likely, they wouldn't have passed to the next round even if they had excellent customer service skills. And on top of that, we would also have gender, age and nationality restrictions, depending on the strategic decisions that top management considered appropriate for the airline. Obviously, candidates weren't aware of these hidden requirements and we weren't allowed to give any feedback either, so most of the times they wouldn't understand why they had not been successful enough to move to the next round, to the point that they could even become aggressive. And that would make me feel so sad.

Our Open Days were very popular worldwide, in fact we could end up having three hundred or even five hundred aspirants attending to one recruitment campaign. As an example, there were some Arab countries like Egypt or Lebanon where we would go every single month because we needed a lot of Arab speakers for our flights, and the number of participants wouldn't vary not even by one, as for most of our candidates, this life changing opportunity would represent the only option that they would have encountered in their entire lives, to run away from poverty and to financially support their families.

But at the end of the day, we were trying to do our job in the best way we could, since the final decision of who would be offered a job wasn't on us. We were only recommending candidates to join the airline and ultimately the decisions were always made by the top management. The airline industry in the middle east was still very conservative and I would even say sexist, as it was still considered that the female Cabin Crew should be beautiful, thin and single. Unfortunately, apart from the usual key competencies assessed in any other airlines, middle eastern airlines would also have many physical restrictions that needed to be assessed like if we were still living in the fifties. But at the end of the day, we needed to cope with that in the best possible way, if we wanted to keep our jobs.

12 LONELINESS, MY TRAVEL BUDDY

Time went by quickly, so the day that I was work by myself finally arrived. That meant, that I would be spending half of the month by myself all over the world. Unless you had friends at the destinations, you would be spending most of your time on and off Skype chatting with your friends or your family back home. Apart from being alone during the whole recruitment campaign, we were travelling alone as well. Sometimes we would be travelling for twenty-four hours in a row if we had to travel to cities outside of the airline flight network. Sometimes it might seem that it could be good to disconnect from everything and everyone, but this amount of solo travelling, could end up making you crazy.

Travelling with the amount of baggage that we were carrying was a challenge. We would pack work clothes and casual ones, as well as the computer, projector, speakers and all the printed paperwork for the event. So that meant: two suitcases and a cabin bag. Since we had to travel to two cities within the same country, travelling in a regional train was sometimes the only option available. As you can imagine, that was not comfortable at all. I had an incident once taking the train from Amsterdam to Rotterdam and I fell when I was trying to step into the train. As a result, my leg got trapped in between the train and the platform. The driver didn't see it, so he was about to close the doors but luckily a couple of passengers lifted me quickly and advised the train personnel to stop the engine. I was in so much pain and my leg was full of bruises and covered in blood. I could barely walk, and I felt lonely and unprotected in a foreign country and thinking that If I wouldn't have had to go by myself, none of this would have happened.

Since I didn't have anyone to talk to after work, I had this need to start conversations with waiters and waitresses when having lunch or dinner. When male waiters would see a chatty European girl by herself, they would be open to talk, and sometimes I would even get wine for free. I even got invited once to a Halloween party by a restaurant waiter in Brussels! Which of course I didn't go as I was always very cautious, and I was travelling alone. But the worse thing was, that I did think of going. The worst thing that happened to me while doing solo recruitment campaigns was when I went to the island of Tenerife. The beautiful sunny island became my worst nightmare. Initially when I saw it in my recruitment plan, I thought it would be fun, since my friend David was living at the island next to Tenerife and he would come for a short visit. We had some tapas together and a great catch up, however I was not feeling well, and I thought I was getting a cold. David left early the next morning as he had work to do.

I woke up that morning feeling worse but since I was alone, I did not have a choice but to finish the day even though I had fever. So, I did the best I could. But when I went back to my hotel room I went straight to bed. I called my Team Manager and explained the situation to her. We decided that the only option was to cancel the interviews for the following days and re-schedule them for next time we would go there. When calling the candidates from my hotel room I explained that I was very sick, they were worried about my health and they understood completely the situation since I didn't have anyone to back me up. I needed a doctor and antibiotics urgently, so I called the international travel insurance. My surprise was when the operator assured me that because I was located outside of perimeter (in a destination where the airline didn't fly), I was not entitled to have any medical assistance, so the insurance wouldn't be covering any expenses. In addition to this, as I was living outside of Spain, I had been discharged from public healthcare.

I had never felt that unsecured and unprotected in my entire life. I was very ill, and I was feeling abandoned by my country and by the company I was working for. The only thing I was asking for was to get some medicine. After arguing on the phone with the medical insurance for hours, they finally allowed me to go to hospital in order to get some antibiotic shots. Tenerife Island, a heavenly trip that was meant to be perfect, became some of the worst days of my life. That whole incident and the slow reaction of the company I was working for made me think, that it wasn't worth it, giving out your life for nothing. That trip was one of the turning points in which I began to think that perhaps the comfortable but lonely lifestyle I was having, it wasn't made for me.

13 THE GOLDEN CAGE

When I had made up my mind that I wanted to go back home, I had been already living in Dubai for seven years and getting out of the golden cage of Dubai was not going to be an easy task. Not because they wouldn't let me out of the country, but because when you are used to a certain lifestyle, it's very difficult go back to normal.

Living in Dubai was like living in a bubble: anything could be made for you as money always talks. The conditions that companies would offer you when moving to Dubai were extremely good for expats and not only salaries would go untaxed. Food, restaurants, and other goods would be untaxed as well, so this was saving people a huge amount of money. Other benefits of living in Dubai was having sunny and warm weather throughout the year, affordable domestic help, private transportation, access to clean temperature-controlled swimming pools, friendly beaches, newly constructed apartments, cheap gasoline, cheap cars, housing allowance and so on. So, when expats would decide that it was enough of this life between the cottons, they would find it difficult to readjust to a reality of 'not being pampered', since no one had as many modern living comforts back home as they would have in the sandpit.

In my duty trips from Dubai to any European city, or when I was going home on leave, unconsciously, I wanted to maintain the same comforts as I had in Dubai. But that was obviously not possible. You would be surprised with the luxuries that you end up normalizing, that outside of Dubai would be considered as something very classist or posh. For example, having your washed sheets or even a pack of cigarettes delivered to your home door step, or taking a taxi on a straight road, so you avoid walking on your heels.

But not everyone had the same perception of what the golden cage meant. In Dubai, there were huge gaps in lifestyle and salaries depending on your origin-nationality. And I am not talking only about the desperate lives of South Asian laborers who were travelling to Dubai in the hope of building a future for their families, but they were forced to work for fourteen hours a day instead, for an equivalent of a hundred and fifty euros per month. I have heard many horrible cases where people who came to Dubai to work, they wouldn't get their passports back for years and they were stuck to the employer on very low salaries, without getting their passport back. Some companies would be confiscating your passport from you and if you tried to leave before your contract would expire, they would make you pay all the joining charges.

When I was Cabin Crew, I had a friend that while going on leave as a passenger, he took a pair of business class headsets from the aircraft without permission and he lost his job straight away. It wasn't a very smart thing to do, however it wasn't fair either to be kicked out from the company just for a pair of headsets. The government took his passport away to prevent him from leaving the country since he had a pending loan with the bank. The poor guy couldn't even apply for another job in Dubai because he was in an illegal situation since his residency wasn't linked to any employment. (Employers usually acted as sponsors in Dubai). So, my friend had to be in a non-legal situation without his passport for a few years, until he could clear his debt with the bank, or anyone could sponsor him.

In addition to the loneliness I was feeling at my current role, there were other reasons that also made me realize I had enough of living in the golden cage. As an expat, we would always be second-class citizen and you would only be able to stay in Dubai if you were useful to the country. There weren't any retirement benefits available and your visa was directly linked to your job status, so your job was never secured. If you would lose your job, you would be treated like crap, simply because employers knew that you needed a visa to stay in the country and you would bend your arm to accept any terms and conditions they had. It should not be forgotten that although Dubai is built mostly for expats, it is a city where the *Sharia* law is the body of Islamic law and all residents must adhere to their strict rules. So, as an expat, you were subject to the laws of the country. *Sharia* law is the law of Islam. It regulates public behaviour, private behaviour and even private beliefs. Compared to other legal codes, *Sharia* law also prioritizes punishment over rehabilitation and the penalties under Sharia law favour corporal and capital punishments over incarceration.

Of all legal systems in the world today, *Sharia* law is deemed the most intrusive and restrictive, especially against women. The UAE has death penalty for serious crimes such as murder, rape, and treason. Drug trafficking also attracts the death penalty. Homosexuality, cross-dressing, adultery, and all of these are subject to severe punishment, including imprisonment and deportation, and for Muslim travellers, a high probability of corporal punishment as well.

The imprisonment experience in Dubai would really depend on your race/nationality, since they would be segmented based on where you are from. Local Emiratis and Gulf Arabs would be in first position for treatment ranking and Bangladeshi, Filipinos and Indians last. Criminal proceedings are long, trials are in Arabic only, and the law applies not only to expatriates residing in Dubai but also to tourists. There have also been cases about tourists who have travelled to Dubai on vacation and they have ended up in jail for behaving as they would do at any western country. I couldn't take the pressure of this city and the job anymore. I still didn't know how, but I was determined to leave from the golden cage for good.

14 MUMMY, I WANT TO GO HOME

I was missing out on Christmas, birthdays, weddings, births, baptisms and even funerals. And then when you stop receiving invitations because most of the times you couldn't make it since the flights were full, or you didn't get a day off, it's not fun at all. But the most important thing I was missing was, my family. I started getting frightened with the idea that my mum was getting old and I was terrified by the thought of what would I do if something happened to her. I guess you think of that a lot when you only have one parent. It was like, I had never realized that every year that I was away, it was another year gone that I could never re-live with my closest ones, which at the end of the day, were the only ones that mattered to me.

At the same time, going home every two months started being not enough for me. I was also feeling that my lifelong friends got used to not having me around and most of them had already bought properties, got married and had kids. And I didn't even have a boyfriend. Not because I didn't want to, but the dating scene in Dubai was terrible. Most of the guys that were living in Dubai didn't want to commit, as they knew that they would be there just for a while, so they were just looking for casual relationships and one-night stand relationships. Needless to say, that the city of lights was full of pretty young girls from all nationalities, so most of the guys were thinking: "Why settling down with one when you can meet up with one every day?". I was over thirty, and I had had enough of this bullshit and I was starting to envy the normal life that I had once run away from. At a lower level, I kind of understood what they meant when they say money doesn't give you happiness. I was feeling very lonely.

I knew that it was time to start thinking about the next chapter of my life, when I started hating everything in Dubai. Each day that passed, the strict rules that we had to adhere to, seemed more and more absurd to me, and each day, I would be more defiant to them, as I was realizing that the whole country was a fake. At work, I was sick of repeating the same lie on my presentations every day, about how great the life and the job was in Dubai. Right, they would get to travel and visit many countries but being realistic, they would spend most of the layovers sleeping in their hotel rooms. And yes, Dubai was a pretty cool city to live in, but at the end of the day, you were there by yourself and no one would miss you or even would notice you, if something happened to you. This was a country where, if you were unlucky enough to be raped by a bunch of guys, you would be the only one judged and sent straight to prison for being drunk and having had sex outside marriage. Period.

I became automated: When working abroad which was half of the month, after finishing the selection process I would go straight to my hotel room and my only excitement of the day was the thought of what dish I would choose from the room service menu and if it was there, I would watch any Spanish or English TV channel available. I came to a point that I didn't pay attention if I was in a cool city like New York or Rome, as the only thing I wanted to do was to be in my hotel bed in my pyjamas. I was tired of going for a walk by myself. I wasn't happy. I was also feeling weighed down as I didn't know exactly what job opportunities I could have back home after being in Dubai for so long. What would live be like after living in Dubai? Where else in the world would I have this comfortable life and good weather all year long?

On the other hand, as a result of not seeing my friends regularly when I would meet them in Barcelona, I was not feeling completely connected to them. Every time I would meet with my life-long friends, I would notice that we had less and less things in common and although we caught up every time I would travel to Barcelona, it was not the same. Truth is, sometimes when I would get there, I would tell my friends that I had family plans, because I wouldn't feel like seeing anyone and I would prefer being in my hotel room eating delicious Spanish food and watching Spanish TV shows. Likewise, the number of friends I use to have, reduced considerably over the years, because as you can imagine, it is quite difficult to catch up with everyone's lives when you live seven thousand kilometres away.

When you leave your homeland for a few years with the pretension of starting a full new life elsewhere, but after few years you start wanting to go back home, you kind of feel that you have lost connection with your own roots because you have made new roots at the country you are living in. But at the same time, in the country that temporarily 'adopts' you and in which you are currently living (the receiving country), you have never had this feeling of belonging to that place. I felt like an outsider in Barcelona and in Dubai. As a matter of fact, I was feeling like I was having two completely different lives, without not even belonging to either. I wanted to go home, but... where was home now?

I didn't want to tell much to my mum about what I was going through, as I didn't want to worry her with my inner struggles. But she knew that I couldn't take it anymore and that I was fed up with everything. She would also advise to me that the current job situation in Spain was still quite bad, due to the global economic recession and having a job with a minimum pay, was a luxury good. I must say that I wasn't fully conscious about how bad Spain was because, when I moved to Dubai, the global economic recession didn't start yet. So, on top of how difficult it was to leave the golden cage, returning to a country destroyed by capitalism was even more difficult for me. My mum would advise me to delay a bit more the idea of going back home, as in the sandpit I had a permanent job, and amazing flat all for myself and a very good salary.

But the poor woman didn't know what I was really going through. I felt like I was in a cage where it would be very difficult to escape from and I felt depressed. I was feeling like an outsider in my own city but at the end of the day, I lived there all my life and my family was there. I was sure that after leaving Dubai, it would be good to go be back to Barcelona. I didn't need to travel anymore, and I was no longer an adventurous person who didn't care about what life would bring me tomorrow. All I needed was what I had always hated: routine and stability. So, I decided that I had to forge a plan, and I started planning my way out from the golden cage.

15 ESCAPING FROM THE GOLDEN CAGE

If finding a job in Spain with the economic situation they were suffering was challenging, finding it with the added challenge that I was in Dubai, was even more complicated. But not impossible. I haven't had to update my curriculum vitae for years, so I had to do it again from scratch.

Looking for a job after so long felt strange to me. To begin with, I didn't even know what my job title was in Spain. It took me a while to figure that companies would use different names to refer to it. I also did not know about any job portals or how I should look for a job online, considering the last time I looked for a job in Barcelona was, when I handed over my résumé to the airline recruiter. In addition to that, I didn't have a clear idea of what sort of company would require my experience and assets, since my profile was very focused on the airline industry. Likewise, job opportunities that I found like my current role, were all located in other European cities like London or Malta, so they wouldn't work for me, as I only wanted to move back to Barcelona.

I felt as If I was a secret agent with double identity. I was on my secret mission of trying to find a job in Barcelona and at the same time, I was interviewing candidates in Barcelona that were trying to get a job in Dubai. With regards to the job search, anyone would think that, since I was working in Human Resources and my job was about interviewing and hiring people, it should be easier for me to go through an interview process because I knew all the tricks and what was expected from an interview. But it wasn't like that. I had been living in a bubble for quite a while and I forgot about how stressful a selection process was and the nerves that you go through when you are being interviewed. It's definitely not the same when you are the one asking the questions and basically deciding if the candidate is in or out than when you are the one who has to all questions correctly at the blink of an eye.

I had a lot of work to do. I decided that I would start with taking a nice formal photo for my résumé. So, in one of the recruitment events I was hosting and while waiting for the next candidate to come in, I took a few selfies since I was already dressed up in a business attire. I updated my curriculum vitae and signed up to several job portals including LinkedIn. I applied online to a few office jobs until I finally got a phone call.

"Good afternoon Carmen, I am Elena Maria calling from *Talentjobs* with regards to your recent application online. Could you please tell me about your current situation jobwise? Are you located in Dubai or Barcelona?". The lady asked me.

"Yes, I am currently working in Dubai, but after being here for quite a few years, I am looking for new opportunities in Barcelona as I would like to relocate back home. "I said to her.

"Oh, really? How come?" The Recruiter seemed surprised about my answer and it looked like she had never spoken with anyone before who would be wanting to relocate from a wealthy city like Dubai, to a city where the average monthly wage was a thousand euros per month.

"I have been living in Dubai for 7 years already and I feel that I am ready to the next professional challenge at home. I truly believe that your company could benefit from my international experience and my multicultural skill set."

"Excellent, thank you… so tell me Carmen… what are your salary expectations for this position?".

It might sound stupid, but I was not prepared for that question. I had no idea about how salaries were in Spain and how much tax they would retain. I hadn't had to pay taxes in more than seven years! I knew that salaries were low, but I wasn't sure in what salary range I would be in, considering I had lots of international HR experience, but none in Spain. So, pretty much I said the first figure that came to my mind. And they never called me back.

When looking for a job back home, more of the challenges I was facing was about the notice period. Most of the Spanish companies would have by law, a standard notice period of two weeks, if you wanted to change jobs. Unfortunately, I had a full month, plus I needed some more time to relocate from Dubai. And apparently, they couldn't wait more than two weeks and they were horrified when I would tell them that I would need a few extra weeks since I was still living in Dubai.

I was not having any luck with the job search and after a few months without getting anything but a standard email confirming that they had received my applications, I started losing hope and I started feeling down. I knew that the job scene was complicated in Spain, but I was convinced that because of my international experience and my good English level, I would have more opportunities than the people that couldn't barely speak English or they never left the country. But apparently, my international experience in Dubai was not worth enough for Spanish employers. I still remember the day when I completely collapsed and burst into tears on a work trip in Lisbon, as I was feeling blue. I was not having any luck with the job hunt, so I started to seriously consider going back to Spain without a job. I had enough savings to live comfortably for quite some time, but at the same time, I didn't want to return under these circumstances, as I didn't know for how long this situation would be.

But just like that, when I didn't have any hopes and I stopped believing I could make it, I was offered a job as Recruiter for a British software company based in Barcelona! I could not believe it! Finally, the Universe conspired in helping me achieve my dreams and I would have the chance to have a normal life like everyone else! Finally, I would be able to sleep at night in my own bed, I wouldn't have to worry about wearing shorts when entering a shop and I wouldn't ever feel lonely again... Finally, after eight years living in the golden cage, I was able to break the cage door and escape to Barcelona on a one-way ticket.

16 BYE BYE, DUBAI

The 15th April of 2015 seemed like a normal day for everyone. For everyone but me. I was happy as a clam as this would be the day that I would hand in my resignation letter. The weather was okay, as at this time of the year it still wasn't very hot, but it wouldn't take too long until it would reach fifty degrees again. That year, Ramadan was due to start around mid-June, but I wouldn't be here to experience it anymore. Yay!

As each day that I would get to the office when returning from a duty travel trip, I would get up at seven in the morning and I would take a taxi to go to work, as I had to carry the suitcases back to the office with all the paperwork completed from the recruitment event. The taxi stop from The Shangri-La hotel was next to my building, so it was very convenient for me to take a taxi from there.

"Good morning sir, could you drive me to the Airport road, please?" I asked to the Indian taxi driver.

"Yes madam. Sure." And he did the famous Indian side-to-side tilting of the head, which in a non-verbal communication means: 'OK, I understand.'

Once at the office, the girls and I would go down to the cafeteria for some coffee and a good catch up. After telling my Managers about my decision, I decided that this would be a would moment to announce that I was leaving Dubai for good.

"Girls … I have something to tell you… I have handed in my resignation letter earlier… I am going back to Barcelona for good!". I basically shouted the news to them, without even realising that everyone in the cafeteria had heard me as well and we were not allowed to behave in a bizarre way inside the airline headquarters building. But I didn't care anymore. I was going to be free! My work colleagues looked at me with a mixture of happiness and sadness in their faces, without saying a word for a second.

"Wow that's amazing! Congratulations my little Spanish!" Céline exclaimed with her funny and distinctive French accent.

"Congratulations Carmen! We definitely didn't see that one coming! So… do you have a job there or not yet? Are you going to stay at your parents?

Are you happy?" Savita, our Indian colleague, would always be asking us so many questions in a row and in a very fast manner.

"Holy moly! We want to hear all details! When would your last day at the office be? We should organize a farewell party!" Kylie, our Aussie colleague would be the one who would always organise all the after work get togethers.

My work colleagues were very happy for me and they congratulated me for going back home with a job in hand, as in Dubai it was always good news. Nevertheless, amongst the smiles, I would notice sadness in their faces. Especially Valentina from Argentina, who had become one of my closest ones and she knew that we would probably never see each other again. But I was that anxious and happy to finally be leaving Dubai, that I didn't even realize at that moment, that I would never see them again. In Dubai, it was quite common to hear that someone was leaving. As it was quite common to praise them when they would resign, as at the end of the day, it was everyone's dream. Everyone that was living in Dubai had an expiration date. But the question was, when would yours be?

I was informed that my UAE visa cancellation would be in a month's time, so I had exactly thirty days to be cleared from everything. The thing was that I still had to be working and I had a duty trip to Croatia, too. I didn't have any holidays left so it was a bit of a nightmare. First thing was to tell the real estate agency that I was leaving and set up a day to return the keys and get my deposit back. Another very important thing was going to be the sale of all my apartment furniture in less than three weeks, since I had to return the apartment completely empty. I also had to unsubscribe from the phone company, cable telly provider, all utility companies like gas, electricity and water as well as cancelling all my credit cards and the closure of my bank account. I couldn't miss any step, otherwise they wouldn't let me go out of the country. And the hassle was, combining the never-ending leaving checklist, with work.

Since I only had three weeks to sell an entire house, I started by selling all the big furniture online and I also participated in second-hand flea markets, where you could sell almost everything you wanted at a very small price. The good thing about Dubai is, that since it has a lot of people's rotation, you could sell anything at a blink of an eye, compared to any other country. Pakistani gentlemen and Pilipino ladies were my potential customers in the flea market. But not everything was a piece of cake. As usual in any country, the most annoying thing had to have been unsubscribing from the telephone company. I ended up fighting with a rude Egyptian male shop assistant which he almost ended up calling security, because after spending three mornings there, it seemed that my contract couldn't be cancelled for a reason I still don't know... I guess I was stressed out and sick of the way, some male Arabs treated women. Anyway, I decided to leave the shop before I was sent to jail forever, so I went again to cancel my phone bill, but this time to another branch in search of a Pilipino shop assistant, as they were way much nicer.

The truth is, that my last month in Dubai went by very fast, so I felt like didn't have enough time to do everything. I was so focused in leaving Dubai that I didn't even have time for a proper farewell party with all my buddies. Plus, I had to go to work every day and I couldn't miss that either, since I had to get my final settlement too. Every other day I was lucky to have friends coming over that would help me pack, and with whom I would share memories and tears in between packing boxes. That was the saddest part of leaving Dubai: as the only thing that mattered to me -and the only one -that I was not able to pack was, the amazing friendships I was leaving behind. Especially my friends Jessica and Laura, who became like sisters to me.

In this life-changing adventure that living in Dubai had been for me, my best friends were the ones drying my tears when I had been through rough moments, and my party companions in countless nights out. We promised each other that nothing would change, and that we would continue in contact no matter what, but deep down we all knew that it would never be the same, since life would take us in different paths.

Days went by and I was not aware yet that I was about to throw myself into the void of starting a new life. In my head, I was leaving Dubai to finally go home, to my people and to my culture. But nowadays, I feel like I did not say a proper goodbye to everything and everyone, after living there for almost eight years. And If I had the opportunity to live that moment again, I would definitely have managed it in a completely different way. But at that moment, the only thing I cared about was, getting out of that country as fast as I could.

But another adventure was about to begin. And possibly the last international adventure I was going to have in my life, the wonderful adventure of returning home. I had spent two thousand nine hundred and twenty days in the sandpit. Eight years where a global economic crisis had started and was still hitting hard in Spain. Eight years where unemployment had increased and where my friends got married and had children. Eight years where I had been discharged from social security and where I no longer had a Spanish telephone number nor a credit card. Eight bloody year it took for some people to forget me.

17 HELLO BARCELONA

In between the smiles and the tears, the day that I had to leave Dubai finally came. I had a cocktail of feelings (and a bit of hangover from the night before), but ultimately, I was feeling very happy to start the next chapter of my life. I was going back home for good!

I had slept at Jessica's place for the past two nights because I was homeless already and I had already sent my seven boxes of belongings through cargo. I didn't have a proper eight-hour sleep in almost a week as I ended up having a few unplanned farewell dinners with my closest ones, plus, I had to go to the office until pretty much the last day. Apart from the sale of the sofa that had been a nightmare, as I almost ended up giving it for free, the rest of the furniture sale went nice and smooth.

While I was passing through the immigration control at *Dubai International Airport* with my heart beating a thousand beats per minute, I was mentally reviewing if I had done everything I was supposed to, before leaving the country. Many things came to mind and I started freaking out with the idea that maybe I had forgotten something, as in that scenario, they wouldn't let me board the aircraft.

"*Salaam aleikum*". I said to the immigration officer.

"*Aleikum salaam*. Could you show me your passport, please?"

The immigration officer didn't even look at me, and he didn't even joke about my Spanish passport nor even asked me if I was supporting Barça or Madrid football team, as they would usually do every time a Spaniard would go through there. Maybe he didn't realize that I had been resident in the UAE for nearly eight years? Being honest, I was expecting a warmer good bye from his side... Maybe something like: "Hey, I wish you the best back home, I hope you visit us again soon, Dubai will miss you". I had been always loyal to Dubai and I had felt as if Dubai was my home too... Maybe they didn't feel the same about me? Whatever.

Once on board the aircraft that would take me home- this time in economy class- all the years that I had spent in that tube came to my mind and any area I would look, would bring me a memory. By looking at the bathroom door, I remembered when I had to take a Russian couple out of the aft toilet as they were trying to make out right after take-off. By looking at the business class cabin, I thought of my work colleague throwing up during taking after landing, as she had too much wine at the airport business class lounge, before the flight.

I also remembered one of my first trips as Supervisor (and after a crazy night in London), I fell in my hotel room and I broke one of my front teeth, so I couldn't welcome our passengers as I was looking like a weirdo! And when we helped a gentleman with a wedding proposal to his girlfriend and we set up a lovely suite in first class full of flowers and champagne. And when I was lucky enough to be part of the crew that would do the inaugural flight to Barcelona, or when I had on board the hot guy from the show Crime Scene Investigation and I instructed my team that I would exclusively be the one taking care of him. Or when we almost got beaten by Lebanese passengers when once all on board and after a four-hour delay, the Captain announced that the flight from Dubai to Beirut would be cancelled. The truth was, I had had many funny moments on board that will accompany me forever, but I had also worked very hard. At last, I would not have to get up at three in the morning and I wouldn't have to travel for twenty-two hours in a row, if I had to host a recruitment event in Paraguay.

The almost seven hours flight to Barcelona seemed shorter than usual to me, since I had spent most of the flight sleeping. My friends insisted on throwing me a surprise farewell party the night before, so I was exhausted. But it wasn't until we started approaching Barcelona and I saw it from the air, that I began to feel excited and nervous about my arrival. I had seen my city many times from up in the air but this time, I was seeing it in a different way. Would Barcelona be waiting for me? Did Barcelona know that I was coming back for good? Would she be upset that I haven't been there for the past ten years?

Once the aircraft landed, the plan was that my sister and her boyfriend would pick me up from the airport and we would have lunch somewhere outdoors before taking me home, since it was meant to be one of those beautiful and sunny spring days. Unlike in Dubai, that it was already starting to be around forty-five degrees Celsius, and it felt like the moment when you open the oven door to take a pizza out.

While I was going through the arrivals gate, I noticed that a bunch of guys were whistling and shouting while holding a pink giant banner and some balloons. I thought, they must be waiting for someone that they hadn't seen in a long time. The truth is, that I was so focused in looking for my sister, that I didn't even realize that the group of guys with the pink poster, were my friends! And they were waiting for me! I honestly was not expecting that at all, as in eight years no one had ever come and picked me up at the airport and it became a normal thing to me, I guess. I felt very happy and welcomed, as I realized that my friends had not forgotten me at all, like I thought they had. But I was feeling odd. I was yet not aware that I had landed to Barcelona to stay forever and that I would no longer see my Dubai friends Jessica and Laura on a daily basis. Now, I would hang out with Vivian, Violet, Samantha and Amy. I was going to live in a new flat and I was going to have a new job in my new 'old town'. And with my old 'new friends'.

"Guys, shall we go for lunch to the beach restaurant in *Garraf* where they make really good paellas?" Amy suggested.

"Sure! That's a brilliant idea!" Vivian agreed.

They all seemed to know which one was the restaurant that Amy was talking about, but this whole conversation, it seemed Greek to me. Apparently, I was the only who didn't know where we were going to have lunch that day. At that precise moment is when I realized, that I had been away for a very long time. And that was only the beginning.

18 FEELING LIKE A TOURIST IN MY CITY

My first days in Barcelona were fantastic and the weather was lovely. (I know I talk a lot about the weather, but you end up really appreciate getting out of a building with aircon at eighteen degrees Celsius, without getting your sun glasses getting fogged!). At the beginning, I didn't feel any substantial changes or differences compared to my old lifestyle in Dubai. I guess I was feeling like I was still on vacation, as I didn't realize how different my life would be. The worst part of repatriation was, registering myself everywhere as if I was just born again. I would start my day by watching Spanish TV and I would drink a latte in my pyjamas. I was feeling as if nothing had changed, as I had the sensation that everything was still the same as when I left for Dubai. But I was completely wrong.

I was super excited about my first day at the office as if it was a child's first day at school. Gabriel, my direct Supervisor, advised me that the office dress code was way more casual than the one I was used to in Dubai, so I thought that it would be fine to go without a blazer, so I decided to wear a shirt and a pair of heels. Still, I looked like I didn't get the memo, as the concept of 'smart casual' that I had in mind from my experience in Dubai, was not the same as the one in Barcelona… I was shocked when on my first day at work, I saw that everyone around me was wearing broken jeans and sneakers to go to work! But nothing I wouldn't be able to fix with a short visit to the shopping mall. That same evening, I bought my first pair of New Balance trainers, which were quite fashion at that time in Barcelona.

I was thrilled with my new life and I was not missing Dubai at all: I was meeting my friends regularly, I was riding my bicycle on the weekends and I was enjoying the amazing range of pork cuts like Spanish ham, chorizo or sausage, that were part of our gastronomy. Plus, it had been sunny every day since I came to Barcelona, so I felt very comfortable with my new life. I had made the right decision. But after the 'honeymoon' period started fading and the summer season would be coming to an end shortly, I started feeling odd. In addition to that, I hadn't been inside an aircraft since my repatriation flight to Barcelona, and it had been more than three months since that date. I used to fly at least once I week so the idea of not going anywhere and not having the so wanted standby ID tickets that you get as a benefit when you work for an airline, started hitting me. The longest trip I was doing now was, a forty-five min bus ride to my mum's – who was living at the other side of Barcelona. Not that I was complaining, but it felt weird.

In addition to that, even though I was at home with the perfect and stable life which I had dreamed of not too long ago, I was not able to recognize the city I had left eight years ago, as I was feeling like a tourist in my own city. In fact, my supervisor Gabriel, who was a British national that couldn't even speak a word in Spanish after living in Barcelona for two years, still knew a lot more things about Barcelona than I did. It was pathetic.

Although I was working for a British company where most of the communications were in English, we were located in Barcelona, so there were times where I had to communicate in Spanish. Sometimes the challenge was when I didn't remember the exact word in Spanish since I was so used to speaking in English in a work environment, so when a Spanish word wouldn't come to my mind, I would use an English word instead, so some people would think that I was being pretentious or I was trying to be cool... What was happening to me? I was feeling like a tourist in my own city, or even worse, I was feeling like an alien coming from another planet. The worst thing was that I was in fact, coming from another planet, a planet full of sand and dust, filled with palm trees and golden ATM machines. I had the sensation that I had been placed inside a time machine eight years ago and I had just returned to Barcelona now. I know it can be hard to understand if you have never lived abroad, but those who did have any experience in a foreign country, I am sure they can relate to it.

When you live abroad for a few months or even for a year and then you decide to go back to your country of origin, you may notice that some things have substantially changed at home, but the change doesn't really affect you. At least in my case, both times I came back from England, I don't recall going through any struggle when re-adapting back home. Maybe because I was born in a big city like Barcelona. Perhaps, I would have suffered more if when moving to London I was from a small village at the country side. Who knows? The thing was, that I had never felt in that way before and I didn't know what was wrong with me.

I could see how the mentality of the Spanish people had changed in all these years because of the economic crisis and I could understand why. In 2013 the unemployment ratio in Spain reached its highest pick, with almost the twenty-seven per cent of the active population unemployed. Lots of people had lost their jobs throughout the years and the ones that still had one, were afraid of losing them. As a result, you could feel that people were very demoralized. Despite the economic situation, the city of Barcelona was becoming very popular amongst expatriates and it was now known as a multicultural and cool city to live in. As an example, marginal areas such as *Barceloneta* or *El Borne* had become a cultural hub and expats favourite place to live. Another example was that the town of *El Prat de Llobregat* - where the Barcelona's airport is-- had a beach now! I was hallucinating.

But what affected me the most after returning home, were the changes I would have to adapt again on a cultural and social level. When living in Dubai, I had to adapt and comply with their strict rules since I was going to live there. And once you get used to it, you accept it as a normal thing, and it becomes a habit. So, I guess I became a bit *Muslimized*. For example, in Spain it is common to go top-less at the beach and pretty much all the ladies are with their boobies out. As an anecdote I can say, that I stopped doing it a few years before coming to Barcelona, as I was not feeling comfortable doing it and I thought that it was totally inappropriate!

I had to re-adapt to new fashions and social patterns that were very different from the lifestyle I was used to in Dubai and that they didn't even exist in Spain when I left. Most of the time I would feel that I was not able to contribute to a conversation, as I wouldn't know about the well-known Spanish singer they were talking about, the players of Barcelona football team, or even the contestants from the Big Brother show, from season nine to sixteen. I also didn't know what a hipster was, or music styles like reggaeton or bachata had become extremely popular, back home when previously it was only heard in a few Latino bars... And on top of that, my friends went from talking about deejays to talking about diapers, as most of them had babies already.

For as strange as sounds, there were some things that I started missing from my old life in Dubai, like for example getting *hummus* or Lebanese bread in any bakery, going shopping on a Sunday or getting everything delivered at your apartment door. Also, autumn was approaching so it started to get chillier. Everyone thought that it was funny that I had to re-adapt again to my own country and they would think that it was the result of having been pampered for such a long time. Even sometimes, they would make fun of me. So, I decided that I would stop sharing with them what I was feeling or thinking, because it was unthinkable that someone that had never left the country, would ever be able to understand what I was going through.

19 REVERSE CULTURE SHOCK

At that time, I didn't even know that I was suffering from a reverse culture shock and in psychology, it was not a disorder that has been studied in depth. It wasn't until I started searching what could be happening to me online, that I found out about what I was going through. The first thing I had to understand was: that home had changed, I had also changed, and I had adapted to a completely new culture. But now I had to re-adapt to another one. Reverse culture shock is not as recognized and understood as culture shock is, and this is because people don't understand why returning home would result in culture shock.

Culture shock is the personal disorientation that a person can feel when experiencing an unknown form of life from the one that this person is used to, due to immigration or a visit to a new country, a movement between social environments, or simply travelling to another type of life. Reverse culture shock is the psychological impact that a person has, when he returns to his country of origin, after having lived in another country for a long period of time. The feeling that this person has, is that he does not belong anywhere since he does not feel part of the country that welcomed him, but when he returns, he does not feel that this is his home anymore, and he perceives it different from what he remembered and no longer feels identified with it. Research has shown that re-entry shock is as frequent, as the initial culture shock.

The first stage of reverse shock is known as 'disengagement', that means, when you begin to think about the idea of going back home. 'Euphoria' was the second stage- and it's about your initial excitement of being back in your own country and others may be equally delighted to have you back. Third stage was 'alienation' and it's exactly the one I was at that moment. In this stage, I was experiencing feelings of alienation, frustration and anger. I was feeling like an outsider and Barcelona was different from how I remembered it. Resentment, loneliness, disorientation and even a sense of helplessness was pervading. But luckily, there was a fourth stage of re-entry, which would include a gradual readjustment to life at home.

When you go back home after being away for so long, you feel as if you are in a cultural limbo, where you just do not fit anywhere. I was trying to maintain a similar lifestyle that the one I used to have in Dubai in order to re-adapt quickly back home, but that was not possible. I forgot about how quickly you could go into debt as my credit card bill was getting higher and higher, as I had forgotten that in my new life I had to pay for rent, utilities, transportation, gym and so on. Since I had to stop doing activities that I used to do in Dubai because I didn't have money to do it, I started making a lot of critical judgments about home and furthermore, this frustration was displaced, often onto others. I was only remembering all of the wonderful things about Dubai and I was comparing them against the least pleasant aspects of being home. My friends began to get tired of my criticism towards everything and my continuous moaning. They thought I had become a high maintenance girl, but who wouldn't have gotten used to such an easy life?

At work I was not feeling any better. Apart from Gabriel who was English born, everyone else was Spanish, and despite the fact we would all hang out after work very often, I felt that I didn't belong there. With the frustration and disillusionment of 'home', I started thinking if coming back to Barcelona, had been the right decision.

20 ROCK BOTTOM

It had been six months since I had been back, and I hadn't adapted just yet. In fact, I was feeling homesick from my old life in Dubai, which was a strange feeling to experience, considering I was technically home. And on top of that, I was also missing the airline environment because the reality was, interviewing information technology people for a software company was not as fun as interviewing young and motivated people from all around the world who are dreaming for an opportunity in a top middle-eastern airline.

As you know, technology is always developing faster than what companies can possibly implement, so Information Technology jobs are projected to be amongst the fastest growing for the next decade. Hence, IT jobs are in high demand in the job market and there is more demand than supply, so head-hunters need to actively search for computer science candidates within the market and sell them the company. Which is opposite of what would happen with any other position where you post a job advert and you get many applicants interested. Consequently, candidates were not really motivated in the event of an interview and they were more difficult to interview as communication is not one of information technology people's best abilities.

My perfect job in Barcelona would have been an office-based airline Recruiter. However, there weren't any vacancies available at that time, so I stopped dreaming about the idea of continuing work in a Human Resources department for an airline, back home. Since I was spending half of the day at LinkedIn 'trying to fish' the best information technology candidates within the market, I couldn't help by noticing other job opportunities that could be interesting for me.

I applied online to a job that seemed quite interesting and they ended up offering me a very attractive opportunity. It wasn't in aviation, but the fashion industry seemed more exciting than information technology. The headquarters were located right in front of the beach and you could enjoy sea view from your desk. I connected very quickly with the team, as most of them were foreigners, so in this international environment, I felt like I was home. In fact, for the first time since I had come back, I had this feeling of belonging somewhere. They also seemed very interested in my previous life in Dubai and during our lunch breaks they would ask me to tell stories about the sandpit. It looked like I gained back the celebrity status of a 'Dubai expat', since my friends weren't as interested in hearing about my foreign experiences anymore. There were happy times, although they didn't last for long.

I had signed for a permanent contract with an agency, so we weren't contracted directly by the fashion company and we were promised to be working on the project for at least two and a half years. After a month working there, I received a call from the human resources department informing me that the contract between the consultancy agency and the retail company had been cancelled, so the whole team was being dismissed from the project, due to disagreements in between the client and the consultancy agency. Since the consultancy agency was an English company, the only projects they would be able to offer to us would be based in the UK. But they didn't even offer us the option of relocation. It took me a few days to realize that I was jobless... Welcome to Spain, I thought.

I had been fired for the first time in my life and I had left a permanent job to start this new project. And on top of that, since I had been out of the country for that long, I was not entitled to receive any unemployment benefit from the government. I thanked god that I had some savings as I needed to pay the rent, otherwise I would have had to return to my mum's place. I couldn't believe that on top of all the issues I was facing as I was not adapting well, I didn't even have a job now. I felt like I hit rock bottom and that came also with a bit of depression, as I felt that I had lost it all.

I was feeling very down because I felt that I had failed. I was definitely in my darkest hours as I had flat-out hit rock bottom -emotionally, financially, mentally, and spiritually. The crash was painful in every way, and I finally had no choice but to face myself brutally, painfully, and honestly. I couldn't think with clarity and I started questioning everything and everyone around me. Was the universe trying to tell me that I had done a terrible mistake? What had I done in order to have this bad karma I was living on, before and after coming to Dubai?.

21 STOCKHOLM SYNDROME

"Stockholm syndrome is a condition that causes hostages to develop a psychological alliance with their captors as a survival strategy during captivity. These alliances, resulting from a bond formed between captor and captives during intimate time spent together, are generally considered irrational in light of the danger or risk endured by the victims".

I started thinking what I could do to feel happier. At least for a few minutes. So, I remembered how I had always wanted to have a cat, but because of the amount of travelling I had, it was not possible. I used to babysit Laura's cat in Dubai whenever she would go on holidays, or when she would have long trips as crew, too. I thought that now that I was back in Barcelona and I wouldn't be travelling for work anymore it would be the perfect time to have one of my own. And this is how Neo, a blue British shorthair kitten of two and a half month, came in to my life.

Every morning, I would be applying to all possible jobs I would find online, but Christmas was approaching, so they were not many opportunities out there, and when I was lucky to have a scheduled phone interview, Recruiters wouldn't understand why the project had been cancelled and why I hadn't been relocated to another one. So, since this was causing me a lot of trouble, I started avoiding that experience on my curriculum vitae. Also, finding a job without having a monthly income was becoming very stressful and I guess Recruiters were feeling that I was desperate, since I also had this feeling about candidates who are unemployed.

Having Neo in my life was filling me with joy and happiness, but as the days were passing by, my motivation to find a job was decreasing. Everyone around me seemed to be busy with their jobs and lives, so I was passing the days with Neo at home because I didn't have a penny and I couldn't go shopping or meet friends more often, since I had to be cautious with my savings. I began to be really worried about my jobless situation after we passed the Christmas period, and the thought of going back to Dubai was present every day. So, one day, I got the courage to contact my ex team Manager and I explained to her about my jobless situation in Spain and about how much I was missing my old life in Dubai. She reassured me and let me know that if I wanted to go back to Dubai and get my job back, I would be able to do it in a couple of months but committing to stay for a long time. She gave me a deadline of three weeks in order to think about it. To be honest, I was not expecting that answer at all. Or did I? Should I go back to the country I was fed up of, so I could have a well-paid but lonely job? Or should I remain here without a job and with the only opportunity to get a job that would allow me to just pay my bills?

Deciding if I was going back to Dubai or staying in Barcelona was a tough call that I had to think thoroughly, since this would be one of the breaching points that would determine my future lifepath. But this new opportunity of having my life back and knowing that I would be welcomed back in the team if I decided to return, came to me as fresh air and I felt alive again, despite the uncertainty existing around me. I was trying to figure out which path to follow and where was I meant to be in the future.

After analysing the situation in detail with my family and closest friends for weeks, they advised me that I should be the one making the decision, but they recommended to me that going back to Dubai would be the best option for me. Having a permanent job was the only way to be able to have a decent life, so if my country was not giving me that opportunity, I had to take it elsewhere. But deep inside me, I hadn't made up my mind yet. I feared going back again to the lonely life I run away from, and I knew that if I was going back to the desert, it will be very difficult to meet someone who would accept having his partner away half of the month.

I decided to call Javier, one of my Dubai friends that had left three years ago, as I was looking for some advice. He had been jobless in Spain for almost a year too, so he would be able to empathize with me, as he had been through exactly the same experience as I did. Javier said to me that I needed to be more patient and soon I would be able to find a proper job. He told me that all I needed was time. He also stressed on the idea that I would regret going back to Dubai and reminded me about the crazy rules that we had to adhere while living there. He was right. Even if I decided to go back to Dubai, I would eventually be returning home again and I would have to go through the same process over again, but this time, being much older and with more difficulties settling back home. And there was also a 'tiny' problem added if I decided to go back to my old travelling lifestyle… Neo was three-months old and he couldn't stay alone for fifteen days a month. And abandoning him was not on the cards.

22 ERIC

After going through the most difficult decision I had to make in my whole life, I concluded that the best option for me would be to stay in Barcelona. Even though I didn't have a job or a home of my own just yet, I knew that my place was here. I knew that if I had gone back to Dubai, sooner or later I would have come back again, because Dubai is a transit place where you can't live forever. I thanked my Manager for the opportunity given and I told her about my decision of not going back. Maybe I had been an idiot for not taking this opportunity again as this train wouldn't be stopping again, but I felt that I needed to trust my gut feeling. And this is when you realize that it's better to go slow in the right direction than fast in the wrong direction.

I truly believe that at that moment of my life, I still needed to learn a lesson and I also needed to appreciate and value everything I had around me. I went through one setback after another in short period of time, and I went from having it all to have nothing very fast. It's not the low points in life that define who we are, its rather how we deal with those low points that define who we will be. No one wants to hit rock bottom but, I guess it is essential that we all go there from time to time, that is the bottom line... Because there are lessons that you learn while you are at the bottom that no one else can teach you..

When I had finally made peace with myself and I began to accept my situation, I felt that everything started falling into the right place again. And just like that, two weeks after I had decided to stay in Barcelona, I met the love of my life.

When I met Eric, I was still at my lowest point and I was feeling that I had nothing to offer to him, other than my heart. And I guess, that this is when the magic happened. For the first time in my life, I didn't have the need to impress a guy, as I didn't have anything to show off from: I didn't have a job, I didn't own any property and I was sharing apartment with a friend at the age of thirty-five. I used to tell him about my previous life of bling and luxe in the golden cage and all the places I had been in the world, so he could understand how I ended up being in that situation. But I think he actually fell in love with the person I was at that precise moment, with nothing to offer to him but my soul. Eric made me appreciate the simple things in life that I had forgotten, or I was unable to do in a desert like going hiking, and he made me realize how going to expensive restaurants and travelling business class, was not an important thing anymore.

I will always be very thankful to him for the peace he gave me at that moment of my life, and he made me the happiest person on earth, as I stopped being ashamed for having lost it all. I felt that I had finally found my soulmate. It's funny, because I had always imagined that I would end up with a different type of person. I had always thought that my future husband wouldn't be Spaniard and he would be working in something international or related to aviation, like a pilot or something like that. And maybe that's why it hadn't worked before, because I did not focus on the things that really mattered in life. And the Universe had a better plan for me.

A few weeks after I met Eric, I finally found a job. They wouldn't pay me much, but it allowed me to continue being in the field and I was gaining experience within the Spanish market since I didn't have any yet. Eric lived 60km away from Barcelona, so after a couple of months seeing each other only for the weekends, he asked me to move in with him, at his place. Neo and I were so happy, specially Neo, who would now have loads of space to run and a staircase to jump from. Those were happy times and my previous life in Dubai seemed very far from us. Like if it had always been someone else's life. But I haven't faced my demons yet, I also wasn't free from the pain I was going through. I still had this feeling of not belonging anywhere and I was still not able to connect with anyone. When in social gatherings, I had that strange feeling that everyone would be against me. And this is when I decided to start going to therapy.

Although my therapist was originally from Argentina, it looked like she had no clue about the challenges that someone could go through, when returning home after living in a foreign country. I guess that maybe because she was still at the expat stage in Spain and she didn't even know yet what would represent to her if she decided to go back to Argentina. Or maybe these were the new first-world problems of millennials? But still, I was amazed how come a disorder that you can get easily as a consequence of living overseas in a world, where everyone is moving around countries and could destabilize your life and lead to depression, has not been included in psychology books? And it wasn't only my therapist who had no clue about it, because I had also asked a couple of friends that studied psychology too, although they were the type that never left their hometown.

But I must admit, that going to therapy did me the world of good, as I was enjoying that I could speak to someone about my feelings without being judged. She made me understand that being back home didn't mean that I had to hang out with my old-friends all the time, as It was also ok to make new friends, too. And if the issue was that I didn't like my current job because I was not connecting with the environment, it was ok to look for a more international one that would make me happier. At that time, I was working for a Spanish pharmaceutical company with Eric- he would be in finance and I would be in human resources- and we would go to work together, but I was bored as crap and I was feeling like a fish out of water as I was used to a more fast-pace environment. Plus, as it wasn't required, I wouldn't speak with anyone in English at work.

"So… why don't you write about it?" Eric suggested to me during one of car rides to work where I would be moaning about life, as usual.

"About my experience in Dubai, or about how I am feeling now?" - I asked to Eric thinking about what he just said to me.

"Both".

23 LIFE AFTER DUBAI

I have always had in mind the idea of writing a book, but I was never sure of what the book would be about. Writing about my own story had been the most incredible experience ever and had helped me a lot in letting all my thoughts and feelings, go away. I have to say, that I found it very rewarding to express my feelings on paper and hopefully my story, will help everyone who, after returning home from the adventure of living elsewhere, has also felt lost at some point.

My experience in Dubai will be with me for the rest of my life and I am very thankful for the fantastic opportunity I have been blessed to live. So that is why, I cheer everyone to get out of their comfort zone and do as many things as they can. At the end of the day, what we take with us in our life journey are our feelings, our beliefs and our experiences. Think about what it is that you are carrying, and whether you need to consider repacking your bags. Life is short, and you are the pilot of your life. Travelling and meeting other cultures is very fulfilling and everyone should see by themselves that the grass isn't always greener on the other side. In my case, I had to travel to the end of the world, to appreciate what I had always had next door. But the 'expedition' to find out about what life is about is an incredible journey. It takes courage to live a completely new life in a foreign country leaving your beloved ones behind, but it also takes a lot of courage, having to re-set your life, back home.

Think about *The Iliad*: Homer predicted about the reverse culture shock, back in the 8th century BC. For those who don't know, the epic poem narrates the journey of king Odysseus' return home after a decade away, when the Trojan war had ended, only to find that once he arrived at his beloved homeland Ithaca, he didn't recognized home as such. So, if king Odysseus was able to be back on his feet after that experience, don't you think you can do it, too?

It has been four years since I left Dubai, and my life has changed a lot since then. I have been through a few challenges after being back and I have struggled to find stability. But now, I look back with immense gratitude for the incredible gifts that time gave to me. I learned to trust that the Universe did have my back, contrary to what I had thought initially. I can confidently say that all the things that I have always visualized having in my life, I have managed to attract them: I overcame my fear of driving and for the first time in my life I am able to drive my own car. I accomplished my dream of working in human resources for an international airline at home. And Eric is now my husband and we bought a beautiful house by the beach. For some of you, they might be the normal things that anyone can achieve. But for me, after all the changes I have been through throughout my life since my parent's divorce, I had been always looking for stability and I can happily say that now, I don't have to fight my demons anymore and I have finally found my inner peace and I am happy to be here, forever.

ABOUT THE AUTHOR

Carmen is a novel writer and an established HR professional within the aviation industry, who was born in Barcelona. She holds a bachelor's degree in Tourism Management, a Postgraduate in Marketing and a Human Resources certification. Carmen has always been passionate about travelling and meeting other cultures, being an expatriate herself for more than ten years. With 'Life after Dubai', the author has premiered in the exciting adventure of writing, and there is no doubt that it will be the first book of many with more to follow.

If you wish to keep in touch with the author when the next book gets published, or if you would like to contact her directly, you can do it through the following e-mail address: *lifeafterdubai@gmail.com.*

○ jet lagg ...

(Austin?)

○ my moms feeling (happy, scared)
with leaving ...
○) day then and now

○ I am just going for ...

○ guide on ... tips when in

○ home

○) ...

○ no ...

○ The ... bus

○ I travelled to ...
to meet the ...

home

Printed in Poland
by Amazon Fulfillment
Poland Sp. z o.o., Wrocław

48990601R00045